TOOLS OF THE TRADE

TOOLS OF THE TRADE

POEMS FOR NEW DOCTORS

Edited by
Dr Lesley Morrison
Prof. John Gillies
Revd Ali Newell
Dr Noy Basu
Dr Rachel Millar
Samuel Tongue

Scottish **Poetry** Library

Polygon

This new edition first published in 2022 by
The Scottish Poetry Library
5 Crichton's Close, Edinburgh EH8 8DT and
Polygon, an imprint of Birlinn Ltd
West Newington House, 10 Newington Road,
Edinburgh EH9 1QS

9 8 7 6 5 4 3 2 1

First published in 2014 by the Scottish Poetry Library

www.scottishpoetrylibrary.org.uk
www.polygonbooks.co.uk

ISBN 978 1 84697 612 4

The publishers are grateful for all the donations
towards the cost of this anthology

Typeset in Verdigris MVB by Polygon, Edinburgh

Printed and bounded by Gutenberg Press, Malta

CONTENTS

III. BEGINNINGS

IV. BEING WITH ILLNESS

V. ENDINGS

VI. TO THE FUTURE

FROM THE EDITORS

Many congratulations on graduating as a doctor. We wish you all the very best for a satisfying, fulfilling, and enjoyable career.

You've worked hard to get here and there's hard, demanding work ahead but being a doctor, and sharing people's stories and lives, is a great privilege. This little book of poems is intended as a friend on your journey. The poems are short, accessible and speak in some way to your experience of being a junior doctor. We also hope that they will accompany you through your working life. When times are tough, you can dip into this book and find a poem that offers you solace or inspiration, or that casts new light on a situation with which you might be dealing.

The art of medicine involves the skill of listening, really listening, to what your patients say and some of these poems will enhance your listening and your learning. Some may give you insight into the importance of looking after yourself. In order to look after and be kind to others, we need to look after and be kind to ourselves, and this is especially true in the era of Covid-19, which has put such huge emotional and workload demands on doctors and health professionals.

In recognition of the transition we've all gone through in the last two years, we've added a new section of poems to this edition. After Looking After Yourself, Looking After Others, Beginnings, Being with Illness and Endings, the final section is 'To the Future'. When the future looks so complex, we hope that, among the poems in this section, there will be at least one that speaks directly to you.

We are grateful to the Medical and Dental Defence Union of Scotland (MDDUS) and the Royal College of General Practitioners Scotland (RCGP) for their generous support of this fourth edition, and to the Scottish Poetry Library, especially Samuel Tongue for his ongoing commitment to the project. Thanks also to Marcas Mac an Tuairneir for advice on sourcing (and proofing) Gaelic poems for this book. Ken Cockburn has been brilliant, as ever, in seeking out the copyright permissions for each poem.

Carry the poems with you and enjoy them. Speak them out loud and share them. Use them as tools to connect with your patients, your colleagues and yourself.

Dr Lesley Morrison,
Prof. John Gillies,
Revd Ali Newell,
Dr Noy Basu,
Dr Rachel Millar, and
Samuel Tongue

PREFACE

There are many things that may be found in a junior doctor's pocket or satchel: tourniquets, a stethoscope, a biro, a tape measure or a tendon hammer, a piece of paper with the scribbled phone number of a patient's daughter who is expecting to be called back. If there is a book, it is often a little medical handbook or manual. Why should a book of poems belong there, you might wonder?

But in the world of clinical medicine, amidst the discussions of scientific evidence and differential diagnoses, poetry can be useful. It can serve as a healthy distraction. In the middle of a busy day, perhaps read while you are grabbing a hasty sandwich and a coffee, a poem can suddenly lift you to a different place. An image or a turn of phrase might shift your thinking. One may – as ever – quote it to impress, to charm, and to connect. Poetry can be a bridge between you and another person. But above all else, it gives one insight. Many of the poems in this slim volume will take you into the world of your patients – a realm of suffering, worry and confusion, with a need for a cure but perhaps an even greater need for kindness. Poetry can be a bridge between you and a patient. Some poems also reflect the anxiety and helplessness that you yourself will no doubt feel at times. And finally, if late at night after a difficult shift, sleep is hard to come by, a few pages of poetry can help with a new perspective. Perhaps you might even be moved to write some yourself.

MDDUS is delighted to provide support for this edition of *Tools of the Trade: Poems for New Doctors*, a little resource for you to draw on in moments of quiet reflection and at times of challenge and uncertainty.

Satya Bhattacharya,
Consultant Surgeon
Non-Executive Director,
The Medical and Dental
Defence Union of Scotland

I. LOOKING AFTER YOURSELF

TOOLS OF THE TRADE

New doctors will be empowered by poems
in the pockets of their metaphorical white coats.
There at the ready:
on early, sweaty, scratchy, ward rounds
to deploy while waiting patiently for the consultant's
    late appraisal;
give filing, phlebotomy and form-filling an edge and depth;
sweeten tea-breaks as if with juxtaposed Jaffa Cakes
to answer that persistent bleep – while sneaking a pee,
to travel the manic crash and flat-lined emptiness of
    cardiac arrest
thole the inevitability of the inevitable;
to pace with careful cadence;
stop and breathe usefully
arrive ready not to recite by rote;
to be alone with on the boisterous bus home
to txt anxious Mums and Dads – 'Are you remembering to
    feed yourself?'
'yes. lol. Smiley-face – perhaps a frog?'
to place strategically on the cup-ringed cabinet – first
    night on-call,
thrust under the sun-torn pillow on the morning following
    the first night on-call
find undisturbed, but at a different verse, following the
    jumpy party, following the first night on-call

to steal insights into the science of nurses' smiles
to prepare for change.
To take a full history, examine closely and reach a working
    diagnosis: 'You are a human being.'
     'The stars sing as whitely as the mountains.'
To investigate with prudence.
To reconsider the prognosis in the light of better-quality
    information.
To appreciate; pass on; ponder, challenge, relinquish,
allow, accept
be accosted by dignity.
To forgive and free.

Màrtainn Mac an t-Saoir
Martin MacIntyre

LET THIS DARKNESS BE A BELL TOWER

Quiet friend who has come so far,

feel how your breathing makes more space around you.
Let this darkness be a bell tower
and you the bell. As you ring,

what batters you becomes your strength.
Move back and forth into the change.
What is it like, such intensity of pain?
If the drink is bitter, turn yourself to wine.

In this uncontainable night,
be the mystery at the crossroads of your senses,
the meaning discovered there.

And if the world has ceased to hear you,
say to the silent earth: I flow.
To the rushing water, speak: I am.

Rainer Maria Rilke
Translated by Joanna Macy and
Anita Barrows

THE PEACE OF WILD THINGS

When despair for the world grows in me
and I wake in the night at the least sound
in fear of what my life and my children's lives may be,
I go and lie down where the wood drake
rests in his beauty on the water, and the great heron feeds.
I come into the peace of wild things
who do not tax their lives with forethought
of grief. I come into the presence of still water.
And I feel above me the day-blind stars
waiting with their light. For a time
I rest in the grace of the world, and am free.

Wendell Berry

CLEARING

Do not try to save
the whole world
or do anything grandiose.
Instead, create
a clearing
in the dense forest
of your life
and wait there
patiently,
until the song
that is yours alone to sing
falls into your own cupped hands
and you recognize and greet it.
Only then will you know
how to give yourself to this world
so worthy of rescue.

Martha Postlethwaite

DEALBH MO MHÀTHAR

Bha mo mhàthair ag innse dhomh
gun tig eilid gach feasgar
a-mach às a' choille dhan achadh fheòir –
an aon tè, 's dòcha,
a dh'àraich iad an-uiridh,
's i a' tilleadh a-nist le a h-àl.

Chan e gràs an fhèidh fhìnealta
a' gluasad thar na leargainn
a leanas ri m' inntinn, no fòs
a dà mheann, crùbte còmhla,
ach aodann mo mhàthar, 's i a' bruidhinn,
is a guth, cho toilicht', cho blàth.

Meg Bateman

PICTURE OF MY MOTHER

My mother was telling me
that a hind comes every evening
out of the wood into the hay-field –
the same one, probably,
they fed last year,
returning now with her young.

It isn't the grace of the doe,
moving across the slope
that lingers in my mind, nor yet
the two fawns huddled together,
but my mother's face as she spoke,
and her voice, so excited, so warm.

Meg Bateman
Translated by the author

from AUGURIES OF INNOCENCE

To see a World in a Grain of Sand
And a Heaven in a Wild Flower
Hold Infinity in the palm of your hand
And Eternity in an hour

William Blake

INDELIBLE, MIRACULOUS

friend, think of your breath
on a cold pane of glass

you can write your name there
with an outstretched finger

or frosted, untouched grass
in the early morning, a place

where you can dance alone
leave your footprints there

a deep pool of silver water
waits for you to make waves

the beach is clean after the storm
the tide has washed away yesterday

we all matter, we are all
indelible, miraculous, here

Julia Darling

LOVE AFTER LOVE

The time will come
when, with elation
you will greet yourself arriving
at your own door, in your own mirror
and each will smile at the other's welcome,

and say, sit here. Eat.
You will love again the stranger who was your self.
Give wine. Give bread. Give back your heart
to itself, to the stranger who has loved you

Derek Walcott

TALKING TO THE FAMILY

My white coat waits in the corner
like a father.
I will wear it to meet the sister
in her white shoes and organza dress
in the live of winter,

the milkless husband
holding the baby.

I will tell them.

They will put it together
and take it apart.
Their voices will buzz.
The cut ends of their nerves
will curl.

I will take off the coat,
drive home,
and replace the light bulb in the hall.

John Stone

WILD GEESE

You do not have to be good.
You do not have to walk on your knees
for a hundred miles through the desert, repenting.
You only have to let the soft animal of your body
   love what it loves.
Tell me about despair, yours, and I will tell you mine.
Meanwhile the world goes on.
Meanwhile the sun and the clear pebbles of the rain
are moving across the landscapes,
over the prairies and the deep trees,
the mountains and the rivers.
Meanwhile the wild geese, high in the clean blue air,
are heading home again.
Whoever you are, no matter how lonely,
the world offers itself to your imagination,
calls to you like the wild geese, harsh and exciting –
over and over announcing your place
in the family of things.

Mary Oliver

II. LOOKING AFTER OTHERS

WHAT I WOULD GIVE

What I would like to give them for a change
is not the usual prescription with
its hubris of the power to restore,
to cure; what I would like to give them, ill
from not enough of laying in the sun
not caring what the onlookers might think
while feeding some banana to their dogs –
what I would like to offer them is this,
not reassurance that their lungs sound fine,
or that the mole they've noticed change is not
a melanoma, but instead of fear
transfigured by some doctorly advice
I'd like to give them my astonishment
at sudden rainfall like the whole world weeping,
and how ridiculously gently it
slicked down my hair; I'd like to give them that,
the joy I felt while staring in your eyes
as you learned epidemiology
(the science of disease in populations),
the night around our bed like timelessness,
like comfort, like what I would give to them.

Rafael Campo

BEDSIDE TEACHING

No one steps forward
We look at the floor, he picks
Me. What can you feel?

Tentatively, I
Press down on her abdomen
The loose skin, lost curves

Hard and craggy ruins
Beneath. My heart sinks into
Her diseased belly

No time left to think
What is your diagnosis?
Don't make me say it

Everybody knows
What is your diagnosis?
Not in front of her

He watches me burn
I won't say Cancer. Not here
Think hard. It could be . . .

Eyebrows raised, eyes turn

I need a technical term
It escapes like a

Mouse dropped by a cat
It could be a malignancy.
And I am a fool.

Mitotic disease
He corrects. We must employ
Some euphemisms.

Rachel Bingham

ANNE TRIES TO EXPLAIN HOW CHRONIC FATIGUE FEELS

You *wake-up-crying-tired*, after nine hours asleep, but
       want-a-cup-of-tea tired
has no energy to move, or lift a kettle, and no tea bags, being
       too-tired-to-shop-online.

Trembling-arm-tired and *jelly-leg-tired* come with that strange heavy
       chest pain
like a stitch from running, except you can't run, which hurts in
       a different way.

Treacle-brain-tired fuddles words – not fridge, not cooker, that shiny
       silver thing
you boil water in – it speaks, hears that it's wrong, but can't make
       it right.

Vision-tired makes printed text slab and fuzz, and glaring
fluorescent strip-lights mean you pack sunglasses for going to
   Tesco.

Adrenaline-tired slumps you in your wheelchair, while thoughts
       rowdy-dowdy
like a jackdaw in a chimney.

Hour-glass-tired feels the sand slip, and all the energy you don't

have, and the years
you can't use, spill faster and faster, and there's no big turnaround

no help, no support, very little research, and no reason not to feel
fucked.

Sue Norton

MAMMOGRAM

'They're benign,' the radiologist says,
pointing to specks on the x-ray
that look like dust motes
stopped cold in their dance.
His words take my spine like flame.
I suddenly love
the radiologist, the nurse, my paper gown,
the vapid print on the dressing room wall.
I pull on my radiant clothes.
I step out into the Hanging Gardens, the Taj Mahal,
the Niagara Falls of the parking lot.

Jo McDougall

A BRIEF FORMAT TO BE USED WHEN CONSULTING WITH PATIENTS

The patient will talk.

The doctor will talk.

The doctor will listen while
the patient is talking.

The patient will listen while
the doctor is talking.

The patient will think that the doctor
knows what the doctor is talking about.

The doctor will think that the patient
knows what the patient is talking about.

The patient will think that the doctor
knows what the patient is talking about.

The doctor will think that the patient
knows what the doctor is talking about.

The doctor will be sure.
The patient will be sure.

The patient will be sure.
The doctor will be sure.

Shouldn't hurt a bit, should it?

Glenn Colquhoun

Dad has mowed the lawn two days in a row.
It explains our lives now – the pushing along

of a machine, blades with nothing to cut –
acting our lives out just to be purposeful.

I got dressed up for a zoom conference
and cried at a kind letter which landed on the doormat.

I need two witnesses that aren't beneficiaries
to finalise my will. My lawyer suggests

I ask my neighbours to watch through the window,
because even with expected deaths the Government

aren't changing the rules. The GP rang this afternoon
trying to talk about a DNR order. I refused,

instead told him about starlings murmurating
and all the living I have left to do.

Hannah Hodgson

THE CRICK

I didn't expect
to be nervous. In
the morning, light
shone through
the coloured glass.
I was nervous,
but happy. After
losing auntie, after
losing my best
friend, I said please
don't point your
temperature gun
at my head. We
watched the news.
We worked 84
hours a week and
only received
a rainbow badge.
He lost his work
overnight. Never
ending screen time.
I've not danced
with anyone in a
year. My daughter
was born. I got

to know the shops
in Wood Green.

Four cabs, that's
how many I tried
to flag down
to get here. Don't
know how they
knew. Was it
my hair? My skin
tone? I wore shades
to hide my eyes.
A snow moon
hung over London
as I travelled
home. It looked
like I felt.

Will Harris

III. BEGINNINGS

MIMESIS

My daughter
wouldn't hurt a spider
That had nested
Between her bicycle handles
For two weeks
She waited
Until it left of its own accord
If you tear down the web I said
It will simply know
This isn't a place to call home
And you'd get to go biking
She said that's how others
Become refugees isn't it?

Fady Joudah

TWENTY-EIGHT WEEKS

We nearly missed her.
This little storm of life,
could have blown by
before we weathered her.
But here she is: sturdy,
definite, pointing her finger
for *this* and *this* and *more*
and more and more.

Lesley Glaister

TEDDY
for a child with leukaemia

Teddy was not well.
Teddy had been feeling sick.
Teddy had to go to hospital.
Teddy was told that he had too much blood.
Teddy did not miss his friends.
Teddy knew the thermometer was not sharp.
Teddy was not scared of needles.
Teddy said the medicine would make him better.
Teddy closed his eyes at night.
Teddy ate his vegetables.

Teddy's small girl lay in the corner of his bed.
She was not so sure.
Her eyes were made from round buttons.
The fluff on the top of her head was worn
as though it had been chewed.

Glenn Colquhoun

KINDNESS

Before you know what kindness really is
you must lose things,
feel the future dissolve in a moment
like salt in a weakened broth.
What you held in your hand,
what you counted and carefully saved,
all this must go so you know
how desolate the landscape can be
between the regions of kindness.
How you ride and ride
thinking the bus will never stop,
the passengers eating maize and chicken
will stare out the window forever.

Before you learn the tender gravity of kindness
you must travel where the Indian in a white poncho
lies dead by the side of the road.
You must see how this could be you,
how he too was someone
who journeyed through the night with plans
and the simple breath that kept him alive.

Before you know kindness as the deepest thing inside,
you must know sorrow as the other deepest thing.
You must wake up with sorrow.

You must speak to it till your voice
catches the thread of all sorrows
and you see the size of the cloth.
Then it is only kindness that makes sense anymore,
only kindness that ties your shoes
and sends you out into the day to gaze at bread,
only kindness that raises its head
from the crowd of the world to say
it is I you have been looking for,
and then goes with you everywhere
like a shadow or a friend.

Naomi Shihab Nye

LUCENCIES

Sometimes, the way words sound
is perfect for the thing they name.
Sometimes, to our shame, they let us down.

'Love', for which we should have found
the most melodious breath of air
such as gave to 'cashmere' or to 'share',
is like a dog's annoying bark, a bore,
'Love! Love! Love! Love!' – until the creature tires
and falls asleep, or we aren't listening anymore.
And as for 'wife' – another canine yelp,
'Wife! Wife! Wife! Wife!' – a yapping whelp
ignored behind a door.
Whoever thought up 'body' for our fleshly form
was plainly not inspired by tenderness or awe.
A dodgy vehicle, this word, comedic, shoddy.

And yet, sometimes, the opposite applies:
horror is wrapped in euphony.
Vicious words that sweetly sing.
What a rich, delicious thing
'myeloma' sounds; a grand indulgence,
this cancer mulling in the bone.
Muted, subtle in its onset,
each darling little cell a 'clone', a harmony

of dark biology, labouring in concert,
its reasoning unknown.
'Death', so soft and moth-like, delicate
as gossamer. And how pretty 'loss' and 'frail';
how dulcet 'chemotherapy' and 'fail'.

Michel Faber

THE LONG BENCH

For the times ahead
when we will be

as if at either end
of the long bench

where distance kept
is love's measure

and death dances
the space between

when words alone
are not enough

and queued memories
reach out to touch

let longing be a store
of nut and seed

that grows each day
in strange hibernation

readying for its end –
the sharing of the feast.

Jim Carruth

EVERYTHING IS GOING TO BE ALL RIGHT

How should I not be glad to contemplate
the clouds clearing beyond the dormer window
and a high tide reflected on the ceiling?
There will be dying, there will be dying,
but there is no need to go into that.
The poems flow from the hand unbidden
and the hidden source is the watchful heart.
The sun rises in spite of everything
and the far cities are beautiful and bright.
I lie here in a riot of sunlight
watching the day break and the clouds flying.
Everything is going to be all right.

                    Derek Mahon

IV. BEING WITH ILLNESS

HOW TO BEHAVE WITH THE ILL

Approach us assertively, try not to
cringe or sidle, it makes us fearful.
Rather walk straight up and smile.
Do not touch us unless invited,
particularly don't squeeze upper arms,
or try to hold our hands. Keep your head erect.
Don't bend down, or lower your voice.
Speak evenly. Don't say
'How are you?' in an underlined voice.
Don't say, I heard that you were very ill.
This makes the poorly paranoid.
Be direct, say 'How's your cancer?'
Try not to say how well we look
compared to when you met in Safeway's.
Please don't cry, or get emotional,
and say how dreadful it all is.
Also (and this is hard I know)
try not to ignore the ill, or to scurry
past, muttering about a bus, the bank.
Remember that this day might be your last
and that it is a miracle that any of us
stands up, breathes, behaves at all.

                          Julia Darling

MONET REFUSES THE OPERATION

Doctor, you say there are no haloes
around the streetlights in Paris
and what I see is an aberration
caused by old age, an affliction.
I tell you it has taken me all my life
to arrive at the vision of gas lamps as angels,
to soften and blur and finally banish
the edges you regret I don't see,
to learn that the line I called the horizon
does not exist and sky and water,
so long apart, are the same state of being.
Fifty-four years before I could see
Rouen cathedral is built
of parallel shafts of sun,
and now you want to restore
my youthful errors: fixed
notions of top and bottom,
the illusion of three-dimensional space,
wisteria separate
from the bridge it covers.
What can I say to convince you
the Houses of Parliament dissolve
night after night to become
the fluid dream of the Thames?
I will not return to a universe

of objects that don't know each other,
as if islands were not the lost children
of one great continent. The world
is flux, and light becomes what it touches,
becomes water, lilies on water,
above and below water,
becomes lilac and mauve and yellow
and white and cerulean lamps,
small fists passing sunlight
so quickly to one another
that it would take long, streaming hair
inside my brush to catch it.
To paint the speed of light!
Our weighted shapes, these verticals,
burn to mix with air
and change our bones, skin, clothes
to gases. Doctor,
if only you could see
how heaven pulls earth into its arms
and how infinitely the heart expands
to claim this world, blue vapor without end.

Lisel Mueller

THINGS

There are worse things than having behaved foolishly in public.
There are worse things than these miniature betrayals,
committed or endured or suspected; there are worse things
than not being able to sleep for thinking about them.
It is 5 a.m. All the worse things come stalking in
and stand icily about the bed looking worse and worse and worse.

Fleur Adcock

FOR MY VALENTINE IN AN FMRI SCANNER

Beloved,

It's because of the way your parahippocampal gyrus
glows green under pressure. The way your parietal lobe
(which, try as I might, I can't see as inferior)
shows hyperactivity when I whisper sweet nothings.

For this alone I want to sail away to your bilateral insula
in a precuneus coracle, drag it high on white sand, dance
the cingulate cortex breathless and wild,

then pull you close and do the fusiform gyrus
as the fiery plate of the sun drops
below the horizon.

You are my frontal and limbic regions of interest.
You alone are my dorsal hypoactive cluster.
You have declared cerebellum on my own amygdala,
o, stroll with me under the globus pallidus of the moon.

Claudia Daventry

WORRIED WELL

Death was meant to happen elsewhere,
in war comics and the plague stats
of History class: but there it suddenly was

in school where Richard, his cheeks rosy
with the bruises of leukaemia, would be
dead by summer, the saying of his name

in assembly causing the headmaster's voice
to crack, his eyes to glitter. Your learning
that cells can riot even in young bodies

unhid danger everywhere: a chance reaction
to gas in the dentist's chair, innocent-
seeming mushrooms dosed with toxin,

all fairground rides likely to fling you
fatally headlong. Always expecting
to be caught out, you somehow weren't:

a backache not your kidneys packing up,
heart not in failure but speeding on caffeine
and stress, a sudden garish rash simply a rash.

And here you are, time's doggy paddler,
the star-thinkers and athletes of your gang
gone under: but even now each dizzy spell

or gut stab brings that lurch, the sense
that any trivial sign might herald
the slow start of the coming cancellation

waking you to worry, to pad barefoot
round the house in darkness, when even flies
are asleep, the morning promised sunny.

Steve Xerri

H E

EYE

CHART

I scowl towards his voice. He says the map
marks how far vision goes. If I could creep

up close I'd learn the journey. His technique
restricts me to a chair so he can track

how far I travel down the chart alone
before I pause. I grope in the third line –

my limit the next shape I recognise –
then stop. No way. I still believe my eyes

can hold a solar system, catch all the lights,
deliver to the doctor alphabets

as small as atoms. But this world is smudge.
I'm huddled at the bottom of the page,

trying to hide my dark. Wherever I am,
I've bypassed every symbol I can name

and stumble at my vision's borders
where letters are illegible as stars.

Nuala Watt

MY MOTHER'S SKIN

When I remember her light-sensitive skin
I think of an octopus trying
to stuff itself into the smallest crevice
tentacle by tentacle, away from the children
in the aquarium hall. They keep
tapping on the glass. And I watch
knowing I'm that little girl and boy
and our mother has just been released
from another spell in the hospital.
They've given her ECT. Her luminous skin
flashes us a dazzling light show. We're scared
but curious as she waves her eight arms,
colours pulsing over her in electrical charges.

Pascale Petit

MEDICINE

My medicine
Has many contrasting flavours.
Engrossed in, or perplexed by
The differences between them,
The patient forgets to suffer.

Leonard Cohen

MY FATHER, ON DIALYSIS

wrote a book about Palestine called
Does the Land Remember Me?

He wrote it in longhand on scraps of paper
as his blood filtered through the big machine

He was not afraid to watch it
circulate

Nurses and aides asked him
What are you doing?

He said, planting a garden
of almonds and figs

Dipping sprigs of mint into
glasses of steaming tea

Breathing the damp stones
of my old city

Pressing my mind into the soul
of an olive tree.

Naomi Shihab Nye

DISARTICULATION

The articulation of bones is a last-ditch language.
Words clamber up to boundless gulfs, and then fall.
And the jangling incoherence of being still cries
to be signified.

That sharp wrist, narrow as a razor-clam shell, is,
for instance, adulthood;

that collar bone's ledge, absent friends;

that corrugated side, the swamp of mediocrity;

that staccato spine, the unlistening;

that shadowy face, the void's indifference.

You'll have seen wandering souls
bearing these hieroglyphs of sorrow.

But who can read a submerged litany?
You look well, we say, though she may be further away
than ever. Her testament, just and absolute,
has been made mute,

bribed to conform to the mechanics of living.
Call it anorexia if it's easier. I'd call it telling the truth.

Nicola Healey

GUIDEWIRE INSERTION, PRE-SURGERY

The doctor didn't look like a Victorian entomologist
as she pushed her forearm, full weight
between my breasts
to be absolutely sure she would bore
into the lump
this time

I felt like a moth splayed in a case,
and no, technically, it didn't hurt
but oh the pressure, the puncture, the pinning.

Jay Whittaker

JUNIOR DOCTOR LEARNING LOG
after Liz Berry

I have aimed bevelled needles between L3 and 4
and marvelled as spinal fluid fell drop by drop.

I have pierced arteries and countless veins,
watched cannulas fill with blood and saline flow,

worried about serum potassiums way too high
and puzzled over arterial gases when the pH was low.

I have recognised ST elevation on many ECGs
and spotted the pattern of atrial fibrillation

and listened to a thousand breaths in and out,
my stethoscope a fixture around my white coat.

I have watched the sunrise over hospital morgues
as the morning cast a cool light over my good works.

I have broken bad news and shared tears of grief
when there's no more to say and no need to speak

and turned away from results that shock
and learned when it's time to let a failing heart stop.

Karen Schofield

INBETWEEN

Between the fall
And falling again
Between just specks
And specks again
A momentary form
Of having existed.
Time.
Between the beeps
And beeping again
Between medicines
Gushing in veins again
A momentary pause
Of having rested.
Sleep.
Between the noise
And noise again
Between two jabs
Breath of hope again
A momentary hesitation
Of having trusted.
Covid.

Raka Maitra

ALL CLEAR

Suddenly sunshine cracks the world. Cut glass.
The windscreen wipers sweep away diamonds.
It has stopped raining. Overhead, a rainbow.
The car skims down a dazzled motorway.
Today, there's no such thing as cheap happiness.
The value of everything has no price.
We are together, warm, dry, safe,
passing the news from the hospital
like a parcel around a circle, carefully.
All clear. Light a candle every year
on this birthday of days.
Every forfeit is a gift.

Sara-Jane Arbury

HEALINGS 2

At midnight the north sky is blues and greys, with a thin fissure
   of citrine
just above the horizon. It's light when you wake, regardless
   of the hour.
At 2 or 4 or 6am, you breathe light into your body.

A rose, a briar rose. A wild rose and its thorned stem. What
   did Burns say?
'you seize the flo'er, the bloom is shed'.

To be healed is not to be saved from mortality, but rather,
   released back into it:
we are returned to the wild, into possibilities for ageing
   and change.

Kathleen Jamie

V. ENDINGS

FOR A CHILD BORN DEAD

What ceremony can we fit
You into now? If you had come
Out of a warm and noisy room
To this, there'd be an opposite
For us to know you by. We could
Imagine you in a lively mood.

And then look at the other side,
The mood drawn out of you, the breath
Defeated by the power of death.
But we have never seen you stride
Ambitiously the world we know.
You could not come and yet you go.

But there is nothing now to mar
Your clear refusal of our world.
Not in our memories can we mould
You or distort your character.
Then all our consolation is
That grief can be as pure as this.

Elizabeth Jennings

NOTHING

Because she is exhausted
and confused,

and doesn't want to argue,
and can't speak,

she dreams of nothing
for a thousand years,

or what the nurses cheerfully call
a week.

Selima Hill

NAMES

She was Eliza for a few weeks
when she was a baby –
Eliza Lily. Soon it changed to Lil.
Later she was Miss Steward in the baker's shop
And then 'my love', 'my darling', Mother.
Widowed at thirty, she went back to work
As Mrs Hand. Her daughter grew up,
Married and gave birth.
Now she was Nanna. 'Everybody
Calls me Nanna,' she would say to visitors.
And so they did – friends, tradesmen, the doctor.
In the geriatric ward
They used the patients' Christian names.
'Lil,' we said, 'or Nanna,'
But it wasn't in her file
And for those last bewildered weeks
She was Eliza once again.

Wendy Cope

ODE TO MY FATHER'S DEMENTIA

'black with widening amnesia'
               Derek Walcott

When his sleeping face
was a scrunched tissue,
wet with babbling,

you came, unravelling a joy,
making him euphoric, dribbling
from his mouth –

you simplified a complicated man,
swallowed his past
until your breath was
warm as Caribbean
concrete –

O tender syndrome
steady in his greying eyes,
fading song
in his grand dancehall,

if you must,
do your gentle magic,
but make me unafraid
of what is

disappearing.

Raymond Antrobus

THE FIRST DEATH

I was surprised
how quickly
his body turned cold
so soon after
the terrifying task
listening to the emptiness with my stethoscope to
pronounce

the first death

how wide his eyes under my penlight
unblinking
how heavy his wrist, how still

how easily tears flowed when the routine of death
the autopsy request
the certificate for the morgue
was punctuated by
a sigh
for the hole left in his family

how much his kids look like him

Andrea Wershof Schwartz

MEMORIAL

Everywhere she dies. Everywhere I go she dies.
No sunrise, no city square, no lurking beautiful mountain
but has her death in it.
The silence of her dying sounds through
the carousel of language, it's a web
on which laughter stitches itself. How can my hand
clasp another's when between them
is that thick death, that intolerable distance?

She grieves for my grief. Dying, she tells me
that bird dives from the sun, that fish
leaps into it. No crocus is carved more gently
than the way her dying
shapes my mind. – But I hear, too,
the other words,
black words that make the sound
of soundlessness, that name the nowhere
she is continuously going into. In every minute
I grow into marvellous things and
die towards her.

Ever since she died
she can't stop dying. She makes me
her elegy. I am a walking masterpiece,

a true fiction,
of the ugliness of death.
I am her sad music.

Norman MacCaig

BEN LOMOND

Thae laddies in the Celtic shirts,
                                   a baker's dozen
lumbering all the way to the summit cairn
the hot last Saturday of May
                         as larks trilled
and the loch-side braes released their midgies . . .

Well, up at the raven-haunted trig-point
(as the sun shone bright o'er the whole lower Clyde)
they unfurled a banner,
and triumphant-sombre, ranked themselves behind it
                               for the photies,
  'R.I.P.' it read, then the name of a wee boy

they'll never meet again. Ach,
would the wean were playing fit-ba
       on some bonny bank somewhere . . .

There's no accounting for it, is there?
                    I mean the low road, and the high.

                    Kathleen Jamie

from CUMHA CHALUIM IAIN MHICGILL-EAIN

Tha an saoghal fhathast àlainn
ged nach eil thu ann.
Is labhar an Uibhist a' Ghàidhlig
ged tha thusa an Cnoc Hàllainn
is do bhial gun chainnt

Somhairle MacGill-Eain

from ELEGY FOR CALUM I. MACLEAN

The world is still beautiful
though you are not in it,
Gaelic is eloquent in Uist
though you are in Hallin Hill
and your mouth without speech

Sorley MacLean

AT EIGHTY

Push the boat out, compañeros,
push the boat out, whatever the sea.
Who says we cannot guide ourselves
through the boiling reefs, black as they are,
the enemy of us all makes sure of it!
Mariners, keep good watch always
for that last passage of blue water
we have heard of and long to reach
(no matter if we cannot, no matter!)
in our eighty-year-old timbers
leaky and patched as they are but sweet
well seasoned with the scent of woods
long perished, serviceable still
in unarrested pungency
of salt and blistering sunlight. Out,
push it all out into the unknown!
Unknown is best, it beckons best,
like distant ships in mist, or bells
clanging ruthless from stormy buoys.

Edwin Morgan

from THE CURE AT TROY

Human beings suffer.
They torture one another.
They get hurt and get hard.

History says, *Don't hope*
On this side of the grave,
But then, once in a lifetime
The longed-for tidal wave
Of justice can rise up,
And hope and history rhyme.

So hope for a great sea-change
On the far side of revenge.
Believe that a farther shore
Is reachable from here.
Believe in miracles
And cures and healing wells.

                              Seamus Heaney

GOING WITHOUT SAYING
i.m. Joe Flynn

It is a great pity we don't know
When the dead are going to die
So that, over a last companionable
Drink, we could tell them
How much we liked them.

Happy the man who, dying, can
Place his hand on his heart and say:
'At least I didn't neglect to tell
The thrush how beautifully she sings.'

Bernard O'Donoghue

VI. TO THE FUTURE

ITHAKA

As you set out for Ithaka
hope your road is a long one,
full of adventure, full of discovery.
Laistrygonians, Cyclops,
angry Poseidon – don't be afraid of them:
you'll never find things like that on your way
as long as you keep your thoughts raised high,
as long as a rare excitement
stirs your spirit and your body.
Laistrygonians, Cyclops,
wild Poseidon – you won't encounter them
unless you bring them along inside your soul,
unless your soul sets them up in front of you.

Hope your road is a long one.
May there be many summer mornings when,
with what pleasure, what joy,
you enter harbors you're seeing for the first time;
may you stop at Phoenician trading stations
to buy fine things,
mother of pearl and coral, amber and ebony,
sensual perfume of every kind –
as many sensual perfumes as you can;
and may you visit many Egyptian cities
to learn and go on learning from their scholars.

Keep Ithaka always in your mind.
Arriving there is what you're destined for.
But don't hurry the journey at all.
Better if it lasts for years,
so you're old by the time you reach the island,
wealthy with all you've gained on the way,
not expecting Ithaka to make you rich.

Ithaka gave you the marvelous journey.
Without her you wouldn't have set out.
She has nothing left to give you now.

And if you find her poor, Ithaka won't have fooled you.
Wise as you will have become, so full of experience,
you'll have understood by then what these Ithakas mean.

C. P. Cavafy
Translated by Edmund Keeley

BEANNACHT / BLESSING
for Josie, my mother

On the day when
the weight deadens
on your shoulders
and you stumble,
may the clay dance
to balance you.

And when your eyes
freeze behind
the grey window
and the ghost of loss
gets in to you,
may a flock of colours,
indigo, red, green
and azure blue,
come to awaken in you
a meadow of delight.

When the canvas frays
in the currach of thought
and a stain of ocean
blackens beneath you,
may there come across the waters
a path of yellow moonlight
to bring you safely home.

May the nourishment of the earth be yours,
may the clarity of light be yours,
may the fluency of the ocean be yours,
may the protection of the ancestors be yours.

And so may a slow
wind work these words
of love around you,
an invisible cloak
to mind your life.

John O'Donohue

ATLAS

There is a kind of love called maintenance
Which stores the WD40 and knows when to use it;

Which checks the insurance, and doesn't forget
The milkman; which remembers to plant bulbs;

Which answers letters; which knows the way
The money goes; which deals with dentists

And Road Fund Tax and meeting trains,
And postcards to the lonely; which upholds

The permanently rickety elaborate
Structures of living, which is Atlas.

And maintenance is the sensible side of love,
Which knows what time and weather are doing
To my brickwork; insulates my faulty wiring;
Laughs at my dryrotten jokes; remembers
My need for gloss and grouting; which keeps
My suspect edifice upright in air,
As Atlas did the sky.

U. A. Fanthorpe

IN ALL THOSE YEARS IN MEDICAL SCHOOL

They never told me that sitting with the dying
was the human thing to do
I discovered that myself one night
behind the screens around a bed
at the end of the medical ward.

They never told me that all the family would want
was just for me to go upstairs and close her eyes
and place a bible in her hand
I discovered that myself one night
in the bedroom of that terraced house.

They never told me that fifty years later
I would still remember the name of the patient
who died before we could stop his bleeding
I discovered that myself last night
awaking from a dream-filled restless sleep.

They never told me how easily I would shed that tear
when a patient crossed the street to shake my hand
and wish me well for my retirement
I discovered that myself today
and thought that was a human thing for him to do.

Roger Bloor

SUPERWOMAN

The first time I saw someone look up to me
I wanted to tell her
You've all made a big mistake

you caught me on a good day –
you haven't seen all the fails
I stumbled over to get here

I haven't really done anything
Spectacular
besides not giving up

– and the wide-eyed medical students
and residents ask me how I did it all
and in my head I say – badly

wildly, stupidly, desperately,
awkwardly, pathetically, barely
did I make it through my training

but since experience makes you an expert
in Medicine
I'm now an expert in getting through

this messy life
of training, and kids, and love,
and fights, and doubt, and failure

because I can talk about it
with a raw, open heart
no longer afraid of what others think

of my expertise
in not being the greatest
Superwoman of all time.

Julia Meade

MUSHROOMS

Overnight, very
Whitely, discreetly,
Very quietly

Our toes, our noses
Take hold on the loam,
Acquire the air.

Nobody sees us,
Stops us, betrays us;
The small grains make room.

Soft fists insist on
Heaving the needles,
The leafy bedding,

Even the paving.
Our hammers, our rams,
Earless and eyeless,

Perfectly voiceless,
Widen the crannies,
Shoulder through holes. We

Diet on water,
On crumbs of shadow,
Bland-mannered, asking

Little or nothing.
So many of us!
So many of us!

We are shelves, we are
Tables, we are meek,
We are edible,

Nudgers and shovers
In spite of ourselves.
Our kind multiplies:

We shall by morning
Inherit the earth.
Our foot's in the door.

Sylvia Plath

NOTES ON SOME OF THE POEMS

'Tools of the Trade' / Martin MacIntyre
I wrote 'Tools of the Trade' in response to the announcement of the bold plan to gift a collection of poems to newly graduated doctors in Scotland; I was delighted when it was accepted for this important book. Drawing on my own medical experience and that of others, I tried to convey the power of poetry to support, inform and re-humanise and its crucial place in the survival armoury of health professionals and their patients.

'Things' / Fleur Adcock
When the first line of this poem popped into my head it struck me as something people can identify with. I was pleased when the unnamed 'things' – our worst personal anxieties, whatever they may be – took on a life of their own. We all recognise them.

'A Brief Format . . .' / Glenn Colquhoun
I love the consultation. It is the high altar of medicine, God and priest and man all in the same place at the same time, no one knowing who is who and someone always roaming around. It strikes me how much is assumed within it and

how most of the time those assumptions are accurate . . . most of the time.

'Teddy' / Glenn Colquhoun
I wrote this poem for a three-year-old patient with leukaemia. She screamed at her doctors whenever we entered her room on the ward. On Christmas Day Santa Claus gave her a water pistol. After that we were allowed in as long as we were shot one by one without mercy. She is well now and trains dogs. Water pistols should be a mainstay of cancer treatment.

'Inbetween' / Raka Maitra
This is a short poem reflecting on the passage of time for all in and out of lockdown; of those admitted for Covid; and those waiting for vaccination. I wrote this in the hospital, looking after my child and listening to the beeping machines through the nights.

'Going Without Saying' / Bernard O'Donoghue
The poem was written after the death of a friend of mine – a successful industrial chemist in his 40s with a lovely wife and three children, who committed suicide totally unexpectedly. His devastated wife was partly comforted by a letter he left, saying how much he loved and admired her.

ACKNOWLEDGEMENTS

Our thanks are due to the following authors, publishers and estates who have generously given permission to reproduce works:

Fleur Adcock, 'Things' from *Poems 1960–2000* (Bloodaxe Books, 2000), by permission of the publisher; Raymond Antrobus, 'Ode To My Father's Dementia' from *The Perseverance* (Penned in the Margins/Tinhouse, 2019), by permission of Penned in the Margins (UK) + David Higham (US); Sara-Jane Arbury, 'All Clear' by permission of the author; Meg Bateman, 'Dealbh mo mhàthar / Picture of my Mother' from *Aotromachd agus dàin eile / Lightness and Other Poems* (Polygon, 1997), by permission of the author; Wendell Berry, 'The Peace of Wild Things' from *New Collected Poems* (Counterpoint, 2012) copyright © 2012 by Wendell Berry, reprinted by permission of Counterpoint; Rachel Bingham, 'Bedside Teaching' from *The Annual Hippocrates Prize Anthology 2017*, by permission of the author; Roger Bloor, 'In All Those Years at Medical School' from *The Annual Hippocrates Prize Anthology 2019*, by permission of the author; Rafael Campo, 'What I Would Give' from *Landscape with Human Figure* (Duke University Press, 2002) copyright

Animal (Mariscat, 2015), by permission of the author; W. S. Graham, from 'Private Poem to Norman MacLeod' from *New Collected Poems* (Faber & Faber, 2005), by permission of Rosalind Mudaliar, the Estate of W. S. Graham; Will Harris, 'The Crick', from *A drop of hope: The Crick Institute*, by permission of the author; Nicola Healey, 'Disarticulation', from *The Hippocrates Prize Anthology 2019*, by permission of the author; Seamus Heaney, from *The Haw Lantern* (Faber & Faber Ltd, 1997) and extract from *The Cure at Troy* (Faber & Faber, 2018), by permission of the publisher; Selima Hill, 'Nothing', from *Gloria: Selected Poems* (Bloodaxe Books, 2008), by permission of the publisher; Hannah Hodgson, '10ᵗʰ April 2020', by permission of the author; Kathleen Jamie, 'Ben Lomond', from *The Bonniest Companie* (Picador, 2015), by permission of the publisher; and 'Healings 2' from *Frissure* (Polygon, 2013), by permission of Polygon Books; Elizabeth Jennings, 'For a Child Born Dead', from *The Collected Poems* (Carcanet, 2012) by permission of Carcanet Press Ltd; Fady Joudah, 'Mimesis' from *Alight* (Copper Canyon Press, 2013), copyright © 2013 by Fady Joudah. Reprinted by permission of Copper Canyon Press; Norman MacCaig, 'Memorial', from *The Many Days: Selected Poems of Norman MacCaig* (Polygon, 2010), by permission of Polygon Books; Màrtainn Mac an t-Saoir / Martin MacIntyre, 'Tools of the Trade', by permission of the author; Somhairle MacGill-Eain / Sorley MacLean, from 'Cumha Chaluim Iain MhicGill-Eain' / 'Elegy for Calum

© 2004. Reprinted with the permission of Louisiana State University Press; Derek Walcott, 'Love After Love', from *The Poetry of Derek Walcott 1948–2013* (Faber and Faber, 2014), by permission of the publisher; Nuala Watt, 'Eye Chart' by permission of the author; Jay Whittaker, 'Guidewire insertion, pre-surgery', from *Wristwatch* (Cinnamon Press, 2017), by permission of the poet and publisher; Steve Xerri, 'Worried Well', from *The Hippocrates Prize Anthology 2019*, by permission of the author.